Blue Saxophone

Rosemary Palmeira

Stairwell Books

Published by Stairwell Books
161 Lowther Street
York, YO31 7LZ

www.stairwellbooks.co.uk
@stairwellbooks

Blue Saxophone © 2020 Rosemary Palmeira and Stairwell Books

All rights reserved. No part of this publication may be reproduced, stored in or introduced into a retrieval system, or transmitted, in any form, or by any means (electronic, mechanical, photocopying, recording, e-book or otherwise) without the prior written permission of the author.

The moral rights of the author have been asserted.

ISBN: 978-1-913432-02-7

Layout: Alan Gillott
Cover artist: Mark Spain

Table of Contents

Blue Turtle	1
Holding your Voice	2
Sarajevo	3
Cargo	5
The Dissident	8
WW1 Memoir	10
White Oblong	11
Depth Charges	12
White Desert Sand	12
Neat	12
Waterfall	12
Gold Leaf	12
Smallbluemobilephone	13
Hook	14
Never Always	15
Woman	15
Round	16
Alfred Jewel	17
The Transparent Child	18
Strands	19
Rothko Room	20
Spring	22
Fragments	23
Carefully Fall to The River	24
Long Road	25
The House	27
Ena Harkness	28
The Meaning Of Green	29
Day of Wind	30
Light as Leaves	31
Kiraly Turkish Baths	32
Physician	36
Lamentation	37
Walking to the House of Song	39
Lindisfarne Gospel	41
To The Hermitage	43
Prisoners of Conscience Windows	44

Blue	44
Black	44
Red	45
Green	45
Gold	46
World's End	47
Pine Stretching Cloud Sea	49
The Gale	50
Yellow Panic Bird	51
Don't	54
The Remedy	55
Painting Jordan	56
Tavern of the Troubadours	58
Blue Saxophone	59

Blue Turtle

When your house has been demolished,
how do you clean the debris,
put things in order, fold loss
into a drawer, like fresh laundry?

If you were a child, and didn't know
about patterns and forfeits of the journey,
you would step out one day, as though any day
and find no ground underneath.

Like a Zakynthos Blue Turtle hatchling,
first dropped, a ping pong ball
into the egg pitcher, pressed down by grain,
you must clamber out of the chamber,
start your odyssey across dawn-pink sand,
nose down, searching for moisture.

Older than dinosaur, fragile as a beetle,
a small slate-blue disc, arms akimbo,
skittering down inside dune hollows
leaving a winding wake like wavy hair.

You must reach the sea before the sun is high,
and bakes the bone house hard;
your footpads flinch on scorching stone,
galumph across spittled shore.

The turtle tumbles into the water,
drifts on the current with sea grasses,
plankton, jellyfish ballerinas;
the sea's skin and sandy bed
are honeycombed by sun and cloud –
like the hexagon markings on its shell. ⁄⁄

Holding your Voice
To my father Derek Wilfred Kennedy Cassels, 1927-1963

Holding
your voice
in my hands;
your voice
given back to me
thirty years on;
your voice, looped
reel to reel,
turning me over.

Such a young man's voice
a tender tenor
breaking slightly;
slow and soothing
reading *our* stories.

Leading us like Aslan
through the doorway into *Narnia*;
little pilgrims on a journey,
via the *Slough of Despond*
to the *Delectable Mountains*.

Our faces rapt, absorbed
in the great mystery of words,
beautiful, old-fashioned,
piercing and potent;
even to the edge of the *Dark River*.

Not just the words in themselves,
but the sounds, the images,
the tone of carefulness and care;
and the silence
that wraps us close.

You gave us love.
Love and *hunger*.

Sarajevo

Sarajevo, Sarajevo

City of cupula, campanile bells,
minaret, Magen David and dome.

The most open city of Europe your boast;
now *The biggest concentration camp* your home.

The River Bosna a trickle of rubbish
Miskin Street a blood river...

Arms and legs go rolling like logs;
a man's shattered stomach hits the road.

Five fag packets buy you a grenade:
lie down, pull the pin and never starve.

The trees in the park cut down for firewood;
even the piano, slowly fed, to the stove.

Teenagers play *Dodge the Sniper*,
running the gauntlet for water and rice.

The artist escapes from his burning studio,
leaves paintings he wouldn't sell at any price.

Christmas Eve, the partisan dines in style
On dry bread and vivid-coloured rain.

A man waits at his door and warns: *My friend,
it's too dangerous – don't come again!*

The Press Building melted down like wax,
a giant distorted spew, an alien fungus.

Sarajevo, Sarajevo

No relief, no rescue, no word from outside:
The whole world has abandoned us!

The parks are bare, the birds dying,
nowhere to perch, not a tree or pole.

The old man dying – his body, heart,
kidneys are drained, also his soul.

Save the rare book, the gold-edged classic,
to burn only for birthdays, for blessing.

The professor who taught youth to love Shakespeare,
promotes the glory of Ethnic Cleansing.

The girl without legs smiles for her family;
to a stranger cries, *Who will love me now?*

Dogs, let loose, famished and savage,
rare breeds and mutations out on the prowl.

The National Museum bombed one night,
blasted: our history, heritage and archive.

We live intensely, our lives crystallised;
know joy in every moment of being alive.

Sounds of the whole world flow from one bow;
the Cellist plays his grief within the ruins.

Sarajevo, Sarajevo

Audience and onlookers stand to applaud;
Sarajevo – your finest performance.

(Based on letters smuggled out of Sarajevo during the siege.)

Cargo

i: Journey

The train shunts, blows, pulls away
from a mother's arms
her wail fixed in time.

The ship high and sharp
will sail to the end of the world
to a new and better life.

You hear voices
black waters swag
with children's cries.

Tonsils bleeding, sea-sickness;
not knowing where or why –
holiday or punishment.

The ship ploughs a straight course
between roots,
across the Reef.

II: Primal

The child cries and cries,
pushed away from the source.

*Whatever I want, always
at someone else's convenience*

*Mother, I need to feel your heartbeat:
please let me strap your heart over mine!*

*Do you remember me?
Do you care? Why give me away?*

I want to hate you, love you
I need you to love me.

This dark hole, panic tightens
in my chest since you have gone.

Whenever things go wrong
I call for you. No consolation.

III: Hard Labour

Eyes flinch in fierce sun;
hands harden with work –
backs with beating.

Dry hot flames licking –
terrors of the night –
I am not myself I am other.

Walking outside of myself
in and out of deep waters
I have forgotten my name.

I wet the mattress again,
because I'm afraid, I wet,
so get punished again.

Afraid to fall asleep
in case the Brothers take us.
What did we do wrong?

Fathoms down
Unfathomable
Loss.

IV: Return

Forty, fifty years along
they are returning, one by one,
defiant, broken, shaking.

Bitter and forgiving,
wisecracking and abject,
hoping against hope.

It was the hardest thing to do:
walk across the hotel lounge,
leaning on another's arm.

The floor opening an ocean
legs almost giving way
to meet *her*. ⁄⁄

'Child Migrants'. Up until the 1960s thousands of children were sent from UK orphanages to Australia in a policy to increase 'white stock'; they had to labour in farms and domestic service. Many were told their mother was dead, and records falsified, mothers were told their children had been adopted. A large number were abused. Many returned, as adults, seeking their roots and any living family.

The Dissident
Irina Ratushinskaya, imprisoned 1982-86, USSR

From the black KGB Volvo, a woman looks out
at falling leaves and smells forbidden smells.
Free smells – fresh-cut grass, mushrooms, earth, petrol.
Going back home! It could be a hoax of course,
to break the spirit, the guards like doing that;
Anyone can stop their hands from shaking

if they try. She won't let them see if she believes
them or not, with blank face, eyes straight ahead;
others have been deceived and taken straight back.
Tchaikovsky's First Piano Concerto
playing in your head makes everything slow down.
They ascend the wooden stairs to her flat.
Five floors. She hears voices behind the door;
but they might stop and turn back at any time...
They arrive: she offers the Agent coffee;
I am after all the victor, not they?

II

She had studied Physics: an exact science;
sought a God whose existence was forbidden;
wrote poems with singular candour,
not submitted to the censor's razor –
judged as *dissemination of slanderous*
documentation in poetic form.
Taken, one morning, from the apple harvest,
to the tedious guile of interrogation.
Informers gave evidence against her
unenthusiastic way of thinking.
Sentenced, to Mordovia, six years' labour.
Igor gives her one last, longing look.
Tell me comrade-judges, has anyone
ever looked at you like that?

III

She travelled alone in the train to Siberia;
Dangerous state criminals mustn't mingle.
In the Small Zone with Politicos,
loyalty and dignity are the code:
women impossibly thin, in much-mended clothes,
hold themselves straight.
They work, but not for quotas, won't wear
prison badges – they are not criminals;
don't jump like dogs to dumb commands;
hunger strike for principle, for justice.
But for non-conforming, the price is high –
thirty-nine days in *Shizo* – Solitary.
Cold, hunger, fever, infertility.
Rather this than the gleaming slope of lies.

Igor comes. One visit in three years.
This is no embrace, it is a spasm of pain.
Everything must be seen, heard and said
in two hours. We learn to say goodbye.
Nowhere is it possible to love more
Intensely, more sacredly, my love!

IV

She was exchanged for wheat and prisoners,
at the beginning of *Perestroika;*
crossed with Scharansky the bridge to the West;
gives a reading at London's 'Riverside Theatre'
pale and serious, Igor by her side.
Her short dark hair cut severely as a child's;
candid brown eyes, a mole below her lip.
She read in her own tongue – round, fruity vowels,
poems once written with burnt matchsticks on soap;
her voice high and clean as a sounding bell.
A singular clarity. The sweetness
of a thrush's song on a grey morning.

(Based on Memoir 'Grey is the Colour of Hope')

WW1 Memoir

She had written to him in Ploegsteert Wood:
You mean to someone, more than anything.
He had pictured her: *You, in front of a fire,
in black and white pyjamas, your hair let down.*

He was to meet her on Christmas Eve,
Brighton. With six months' wages
she'd bought a frilly blouse,
a black taffeta dancing dress
with red flowers at the waist,
a jaunty hat to perch on one side.

After she got the call, she went out
to look at the sea, the waves rough,
twisting like a slaughtered seal,
for the crossing he never made.

She ties him into the belt buckle
that clamps her stiff uniform,
wears him inside her woolen cape,
goes to work as usual, through the rain
walks the bitter white of the wards
as though wearing weighted clogs
takes infinite time on the smallest tasks
forgets from minute to minute what to do.

People try to be kind, but she wants this pain
clings to his verses, his haunts, his faith
goes to Mass – the liturgy and incense
pass though her with drugged sweetness.
She walks in the gardens
the sun comes out, warms her skin
but for now the delphiniums are too blue,
too vivid and radiant for earthly flowers.

(Based on Testament of Youth, Vera Britten)

White Oblong

Between you and me, a white oblong,
suspended across darkness.

The frame, a border and edge
inside, matter dissolves.

White, the space of things not said
as though to name would destroy.

White sun, heat that heightens,
a brightness that sharpens shadows.

White, the season which pulls us
into a burning golden oval.

White, the lake of frosted roses,
the skin of ice that seals the water.

White, the linen cloth stretched tight,
through which the blood bead bursts.

White, the weight of sleep on lids,
pebbles on the eyes of the stillborn.

White, the instant when light crashes
through the glass, into blind grace.

White, the wool with which we spin
the stories that never run out.

White, the opposite of colour,
the colour that contains all colours.

Depth Charges

You let down depth charges
in unknown seas
they detonate
the impact never ceases. //

White Desert Sand

On white desert sand
one vermillion tulip blooms
so red, so perfect.

How could you leave it
to spend its passion
on white desert sand? //

Neat

Your words
absorbed
straight – like neat cognac
into open veins. //

Waterfall

Your embrace.
Like standing beneath
a waterfall blast. //

Gold Leaf

With skilful brush strokes
he gold-leafed
her skin. //

Smallbluemobilephone

Smallbluemobilephone rings its dinky tune.
But it never rings. Where is it? Who can it be?
I scrabble in the bottom of my bag,
between books, papers, notices,
sandwiches, aspirin, glasses,
tissues, purse, Lemsip – at last!
I fumble with the somany buttons:
How does this blimin thing work?

Your voice. You in Sarajevo.
Your voice seeking me out. I'm speechless.
It's raining, sleeting.
You are coming home!

Outside the cutting cold makes it hard to breathe;
but my heart is thumping jumping jack-rabbits.
It's been winter for ever; no-one smiles – it's too cold.
This terse alien stone landscape gets inside of you.

We need an injection of light, sunshine pills, a Greek island.
Everyone rushes, everyone busy. I am always tired.
Always.
But just now, I'm young and irresistible:
I put on my lipstick, in a different way.

My train ride home is truly a carriage
drawn by jet horses, who snort and stamp,
a galloping glass jalopy,
taking me to the Ball.

Hook

Hook that you have in me
thrash and mean me though you might
rage and turmoil me into
white trembling anger
and indignation sleep-robbing
gashes out red but yet

It is that hook
pulling down tight
around the heartbeat
the chafe and yank
the hook of you
holds me hard

I cannot leave
nor let leave like this
I turn back, hate-hurting
blind-crying, disembodied
crushed unbearable
dying the suspense of

find you again
unyielding, yielding
the line so thin is
stretching so the risk
and huge oh!
Immense

Love again as once
holds me in tremendous
grip
the hook
slams
into place. //

Never Always

The sky was never black nor the moon full,
it never rained, the sun never burned
you loved me always being so full of words
we never argued over money or gadgets
few were the good times that graced our table
we did both and none and the result was lamentable.

You were never one to laugh at me,
winding me up till I could have burst
we never made love in the sea at *Mijet*,
nor wrestled in the storm against that rock
I'm better off without you, I shall not miss you
you were never always company.

Woman

I am already making a space
my belly a rich loamy lining;
a warm hollow, a barrel of grain,
a grass-thick valley, a nestful of birds,
a bowl of still water, a whirling eddy,
a vat full of wine, a chalice of grail,
an eye full of tear, a bay full of sea,
a well earth-deep, a bell of bronze.

The whole of my cupped life
is streaming slowly through me,
down the glass-green shaft;
all possibilities and impossibilities
array themselves before me –
I prepare myself to bear a mystery.

Round

I am
round, round, round
as an orange, rosy as a
pomegranate, rubbed with almond
oil, I roll and sway, lodestone inside,
my belly the centre of gravity; ballast
on blustery days. I lie in chloroformed
afternoons, ether sweeping, a swathe of chiffon,
opal-grey, opaque, mother-of-pearl, or languish in
the heatwave, basting brown. Things slide off
my surface as though an India-rubber ball. I
can take in no words or ideas, forget all social
behaviour, and on a clear day, if a piano
should play, I become every note, each
thrumming finger, I simply float
away; I'm the melody,
being played out to
the very
end. ⁄⁄

Alfred Jewel

With
huge black eyes
one nostril curl, blurred
mouth, your beseeching cry
has caught at my heart. Green-robed
tiny sea-god, you swim in lapis lazuli;
white bud hands clutch flowering rods,
imprisoned foetus, you flail inside crystal rock,
fingers claw the binding encrustation of gold.
How you sparkle in your teardrop womb!
You move me strangely. As if some
familiar child were calling,
calling out from within –
Please don't betray me!
And are you the Saxon
King, or the Christ
exile, or my own
unborn, twelve
hundred years
old, who is
trying to
speak?

The Alfred Jewel *is a piece of Anglo-Saxon goldsmithing made of enamel and quartz enclosed in gold. British Museum / Ashmolean.*

The Transparent Child
For Lydia

A young girl, on the brink of growing up
like a royal blue tree spreading against a red sky
she is not of this world, she moves backwards and blindfold
four-legged, two limbed, upside-down, oppositely
she performs handstands in the path of the tide.

I can see her skin like shiny rubber dolphin hide
I can see her mouth like a peony, full of raindrops
I can see her hair like sheaves of corn, stacked in rows
I can see her tummy like a crisp white plumped pillow.

Her arms are like stick insects dancing to Swan Lake
her body is a cello that sounds in the belly of amber
her fingers are piano keys running in relays
her heart is a drum kit that she beats all day long
like the tap and tussle of two squirrels at play.

Her eyes are Siamese cats that climb to the highest branch
her voice is the tinkling of crystal glasses which chink together
her brain is a dream of one-eyed aliens come to paint the earth
what a bottle of perfume with the stopper off, the world is to her.

(After Peter Redgrove 'The Transparent Baby')

Strands

A threefold cord shall not easily be broken,
Ecclesiastes 4:12

Tightly twined at the top,
the strands smooth and inseparable
shape themselves by each other.
Tied together for a long time,
deformed by increasing pressure
the strands graze against each other.

One wears thin, roughened
and split, slips its grip
another grows a knot, choking
searing, forming scorch marks.
The third, now visible,
now invisible,
alone is strong and true.

Two may hold, hold
the third in its falling.
One alone may serve
when both are pulling apart
to undo the tired tangle
slowly braid the strands again,
one around another.

Keep the unique pattern
still in place.

Rothko Room

Nine huge canvasses hang here
set apart in this room of silence
maroon on black, black on maroon
darkness on blood, blood on the dark.

      A vertical slab, a pillar of night
      a simmering gash on a giant square
      maroon on dark red, dark red on maroon
      a damson melancholy, an ache inside.

            Dark chocolate on coffee earth
            tan on dark brown, gloss on opaque
            mulberry, bilberry, blackcurrant
            a trodden out late vintage.

            It takes your breath away: sadness
            overwhelms yet the space sets you free
            each can find their own darkness
            sit with it and slowly lose the fear.

      Some people break down and weep
      like you, when you painted these;
      have a spiritual encounter, see visions
      their soul opened up, exposed yet held.

      Destined for a chic New York restaurant
      you decided you couldn't sell yourself
      to wealthy diners to discuss or ignore
      darkness on blood, blood on the dark.

You let go a commission of two million dollars
gave the paintings to Britain, with thanks to Turner
where they wait and brood, breathe and move
in a place apart, a meditation beyond darkness. ⁄⁄

Spring

Spring has never been so rich, so long, so full
day by day the trees wear more clothes.

Toxins seep through, inflame each membrane
an alien buzzing, muffling all edges.

A scroll of birdsong unrolls,
shreds out from the open throat of morning.

My face, soft and porous as iris-skin
lolls towards the light, drinks it.

Fatigue knocks me like an iron bar
painkillers can't get the ache out.

A magnolia opens its ivory and mauve petals
gradually, until it eclipses the house.

A pair of doves fly past my window
their white fantails flash as they grip the sill.

Beneath the cherry tree a thick carpet grows
the wind shakes showers of pink confetti.

A fringed cloud slants across the sky
like a Tyrolean hat feather on turquoise.

Fragments

Beneath the water my voice falters,
muffled, distant.

After a consultation,
we drive past a field,
blinding green bliss.

Parallel universe:
I'm in a lift going down but remaining
at the top.

This is my body,
but I'm not in my clothes,
and this skin is not mine.

I can't move, stay in bed.
watch opera and get lost inside *Aida*.

I am throwing clothes
at the wardrobe handles –
keep missing.

In your mind I wear
a long white dress
spin and spin.

I dream of a golden bowl:
clamber and slip over the rim
lie there, dissolving in the Joy.

Carefully Fall to The River
Chinese Road sign at top of steep river bank

Clear away the debris, remove all rocks;
   take only what is absolutely needful;

A warm blanket of whispering, the hands
   of kindness; a scroll, a mantle.

Time slows down, one minute
   could be one hour, decades pass.

Sand slips between one island and another:
   an attenuation of glass.

I don't know where I am, says Alice
I've changed so many times since this morning.

The body's a mine shaft, an electrical current
   a spiral of heat that twists through humming.

Words come from a long way away, slurred
   dropping down, refracted underwater,

Carefully fall: tip with care, roll slowly
   surge with the rhythm of the river.

Long Road

Pain is a long road
with milestones along the way.

A sealed-off level
between earth and water.

A remote country,
with tedious border crossings.

Or a rocky island they row you out to
leave you marooned.

Time, shunted into a siding
only let out for short distances.

An invasion that jolts me
fallen asleep upright.

My chest, side and back
fixed within scaffolding.

A *Brazilian Blue* butterfly,
pinioned to a corkboard.

Climbing *Hill Difficulty*,
knees gashed on jagged octagons.

Always impelled upwards, or falling away
from the cliff edge.

A carnivorous plant sucks away thought,
memory, energy; disgorges them, out of place.

Beneath the sea surface
the jelly-fish sting sears the skin.

Two women snap the sheet tight
before they fold it.

The blue diamond pill comes every four hours
a stallion that rides the top of the ridge.

I wake at 4am, for once free of the clamp,
I turn and embrace you, as though for the first time. ⁄⁄

The House
Old Granary, Barn Conversion, 1876

Start up this lane, you reach a new domain.
Solid walls but no roof – we bought a ruin.
Time has stopped; it is hard to leave again.

The house is too big. I still need to grow
I sleep with a hat, but my cheeks are cold.
Start up this lane, you reach a new domain.

The wind howls – it's got a ghost of its own.
You're away. *Please come home, I'm scared* – I phone.
Time has stopped; it is hard to leave again.

The house is big. Owls shudder the window locks.
You bring machines, dreams, pipes, instruments, clocks.
Start up this lane, you reach a new domain.

The house is itself, the pillars leaf-entwined
you're here for a season, your words are kind.
Time has stopped; it is hard to leave again.

The house is alive. Friends come, children call;
blue turtle puppets perch on the garden wall.
Start up this lane, you reach a new domain.

Three deer run across the path, bob white tails
two swans swim upriver, their wings are sails.
Start up this lane, you reach a new domain.
Time has stopped; it is hard to leave again.

Ena Harkness

I am a vintage rose
full-bodied, mature.

Not with a young, jaunty scent
but rich, heady, drunken.

Sturdy, long-lasting, resilient
I bloom again and again.

Each petal, a soft, bruised darkness
veined with knowledge of life.

Each thorn is large and thick
but few, and easily visible.

Incomparable in dignity
indescribable in beauty.

I would give you this rose:
Burgundy red, perfect.

Dark velvet outer petals
fine crimson inner petals.

Scrolling out from the raw,
heavy-scented scarlet core.

A connoisseur's choice.

The Meaning Of Green
(Loch Erne, County Fermanagh)

The airport posters declare:
*You've never known the meaning of green
until you've visited Ireland.*

This green so much greener, so alive,
and so many different kinds of green:
reed, sedge, heather-green and herb
ice-green, peppermint, silver-green, sage
sap green, grass, sorrel green, apple
sea-green, mallard, weed-green, brine
stone-green, olive, ochre, khaki
oak leaf and pinewood, willow, chestnut
shamrock, leprechaun, cool as cucumber
orange green, turquoise, aquamarine
angelica, chartreuse, leek, asparagus
bottle-green, moss, viridian, verdigris
bog green, chocolate green, lemon, lime,
mauve-green, malachite, green amber.

And sometimes – in the sunlight,
beneath the green-black lakewater –
pure green-gold.

Day of Wind

Wind skewers the air
it blasts, scours, flays, undoes time;
love's blown clean as bone.

The wind is running
it knocks the bird from its perch
yanks thread from flesh.

All day, the deluge
drives away debris and sun
summer's comfort gone.

The wind growls, famished
pylon lines have snapped, links cut
great trees have fallen.

The cats carry in their prey:
mice, moles, a great blackbird
I clean up blood and viscera.

Better the wind's chase
that winnows the chaff from the grain,
than the stagnant pond. ⧫

Light as Leaves
Beverley Minster

I had never seen the Minster by night.
We came for a Farewell: hymns, a sermon, tributes.
Toasts to the minister and his wife, leaving
to serve the Chaco Indian tribes.
When the formalities were over
and the polite people had left – the party began.
They were few, but the dancers took over –
swinging all evening to Mambo and Bossanova,
while disco lights flicked off Gothic arches.

All that night I dreamed I saw the two of them -
light as leaves, as birds, as the skin of water
rising from the flagstones, floating on the upstream,
pinioned against the Gentian blue of the rose windows,
dipping beneath the pointed archways,
drawn up to the vaulted ceiling.

This chamber, this womb
this sanctuary, this refuge.

Like Chagall lovers, embracing in electric green,
or Spencer's saints nudging their tombstones open;
divested of weight, rising on a song
caught on a lightstream
on a vivid cry
light as leaves
like love.

Kiraly Turkish Baths
16th C. Ottoman Baths, Budapest, Ladies' Day

I

Having run the gauntlet of pinafored matrons,
selling, marking off and taking in tickets
signalled to undress in a wooden cubicle
I walk barefoot down long corridors
wearing only a coarse linen sheet
down two flights of stone stairs
under three arches, through an anteroom
to arrive at the vast central chamber:
a domed cavern, dim and echoing
at its heart a green octagonal pool.

II

I enter the water, naked
it's another world, soundless
without rain or wind
without strong light
the body loses its contours
the mind its hard edges
extending out into the whole pool
there's no separation.

I am so tired that it hurts
shoulder blades are tense
as stegosaurus spikes.
Steam rises from the dense water
along with low babbling voices
the relief is so great I cry.

III

Wall gaslights are crescent moons
that brood over the pool
burnt orange and lime gold windows
send triangles dancing across the water.

The walls are stained rust and beige
with a black comet's feathered trail;
the floor is laid with slabs of scuffed marble,
brown-veined and mottled puce.

The olive green water smells of sulphur,
iodine, yeast, beer, incense;
small round apertures line the dome,
tilting sunlight stilts into the darkness.

IV

This is the domain of the crones
beauty's rules are overturned:
it's okay to be old or imperfect
brown wrinkled skin, and white hair
melon breasts with huge aureoles,
swollen bellies, rolls of flesh
gaunt and hunched, it matters not at all.
Our skins soften, loosen
plumping into translucence
beauty starts to grow inside.

In the pool, we stretch out like starfish
breasts float to the top,
toes, knees and noses peep,
hair spreads and waves like seaweed.
Skin glistens in the dim light.
I swim, I float, I twist, I stretch,
a foetus in the womb
a baby being rocked to sleep,
ballerina jetes in slow motion.

V

Water gushes from a black pipe:
like runners charging up and down my back
unclenches my neck, pounds chest,
two jets tripping over the nipples.

The Hot Plunge: you don't think it's possible
to accustom yourself, yet you stay in
a blue lobster slowly simmering
boiling up, till red and breathless.

Sway to the Cold Plunge, a baptismal pool
your hot body warms the water;
cleansing, cathartic, shocking
then back to the warm green core.

The Steam Room's a dark Sahara
with a dry vapour that rasps and scorches
hot knives chop your skin
fists pummel on a metallic roof.

I peer through a wall of fog
run for the door, almost unconscious
grab the bronze doorknob,
stagger out choking, faint.

From hot to cold to warm to cold
to hot to cold to warm again
we weave a star shape between the pools
always returning to the Octagon.

VI

I watch the windows – they are stars
I let them speak to me, a message from each
a silent reaching, God whispers,
I will be a Shield about you.
A lover's voice, a cry from a child:
You haven't lost me, but.

I'm rocked
bent backwards, stretched out
I feel the love
becoming whole.

Physician
Icon, Lake Ohrid, Macedonia

The background is a burnished orange
a honeycomb cell's liquid centre
with clusters of opaque amber at the edges;
so many layers, aged skins of gold
thick as candlewax, cross-hatched,
delicate as insect wings, veined brown
dark shows through eggshell craquelure
it is both substance and translucence
changing colour over time, imbued
impressed with a living person.

Sveti Naum, St Nahum, the Physician,
Healer of the troubled in Mind
your hands aromatic with bergamot
and herbs, balm for anguish and turmoil.
Today doves alight, nest and fly away
from your tawny honeycomb domes;
you built your monastery here,
on the banks of this clear silk lake;
sweet waters, tiny bubbling springs,
where folk still come to drink and bathe.

The more you look, the face grows,
concentrating with shadow,
as though drawing darkness into itself;
something decreasing, something increasing,
as alchemy's passionate labour
distils dross from gold
and a rich orange-ochre glow
spreads slowly from inside to out.
Is this the tone of love,
the texture of spirit?

Lamentation
Fresco, St Pantelijmon, Nerezi, Macedonia

Mary embraces her son, lifted down,
she holds him upon her lap, stretched full,
legs impossibly bent beneath this weight;
her feet touching each other sole to sole,
her right arm behind his neck, her left arm
clasped across his chest: she raises his head
to her cheek and looks deeply into him.
Was it for this she bore him? Word made flesh,
now a sword forever twisting inside;
her eyebrows are furrowed ridges of earth;
her eyes are smudged, brown darts run down her cheeks,
she receives him in death as in his birth,
embracing, like a mother, or lover;
the moment seems to go on forever.

He lies on a white and gold winding sheet,
his body pale yellow, elongated,
wearing a white loincloth with v-shaped folds
every rib, muscle and bone highlighted
peaceful in death, his face noble and strong,
his hair fine, mouth grave, eyes slanted.
In green hills, cream mountains, cobalt sky,
he lies lifted, as though levitated.
John, the Beloved friend, clutches
his master's left hand to his cheek, you see
how he is stricken, by the extreme lean
of his back over the immobile body,
devotion and disbelief, aching prayer,
absurd hope mingled with abject despair.

Three angels wipe their tears on bell sleeves,
two more disciples bow over his feet
which they hold reverently in their hands,
while tears run down their beards without heed.
A pitcher of ointment waits to the side,

to watch and anoint the dead is a fine art:
to wrap the body up in fine linen.
The Magdalene reaches out from her heart.
To be so loved, so mourned. Not just by friends
or relatives, but faithful followers
down centuries, by this fresco artist.
But how did he know it would feel like this?
Even knowing the ending,
We feel the pity of it – Pieta. ⁄⁄

Walking to the House of Song
Banja Luka, Post-war Bosnia, 1999

Between the end of longing and its beginning
a stranger, not knowing how to find the place
I walked to find the House of Singing.

Though I knew it was near, I couldn't see it, looking
down wide streets, tall buildings, green space
between the end of longing and its beginning

I saw people lean and hungry, they were dreaming
aloud and furious, visions they couldn't erase
yet I walked to find the House of Singing.

I walked through my fatness, I walked through my sleeping
found the Dictionary of the Khazars, history of a tribe
lost, between the end of longing and its beginning.

I passed sleek strollers, to the beggar they said *Nothing"*
Through the skins of age, though the debris of disgrace
I walked and walked, to find the House of Singing.

I saw the sacred next to the profane, St George fighting
the Dragon, in a desperate primordial embrace
between the end of longing and its beginning
I walked to find the House of Singing.

Between the end of longing and its beginning
the Vrbas river rushes wild and turbulent
as I walk to find the House of Singing.

I met Lubitza, the lady who loved the wounded children
healing their anger, sadness and shameface
between the end of longing and its beginning.

A young man spoke, whose pride was aching
he thought he wore the devil's horns and grimace
he also walked to find the House of Singing.

At last, I heard, through the trees, the deep bells ringing
rich tones of tenor, baritone and bass
between the end of longing and its beginning.

The artist painted deformity and minds exploding
the shadow of Christ covered the dead with grace
they walked to find the House of Singing.

Above the treetops I saw a copper dome shining
the crowd were held rapt within a crown of praise
between the end of longing and its beginning
I walked, I found the House of Singing.

Lindisfarne Gospel

Eadfrith the Scribe prepares his tools
first he takes some calf hide parchment
tanned, tightened to the exact thinness
then he carefully mixes up each pigment:
indigo from Indian plant roots
ground up malachite for green
azurite for royal blue, lapis lazuli
from the Himalayas for ultramarine
and from the earth, red and yellow ochre,
raw sienna, burnt umber, magenta.

With the fine point of a goose quill
he pricks my pages, each minute spill
of tincture, is a suture, cicatrice
the rubricator's drops form a roundel
In the beginning was the Word
then he paints me with a pine marten brush
dog and dragon at the edges of letters,
cormorants, the braided necks of wild geese
eight birds inside an elongated wildcat,
three-legged pelta, a flourish of trumpet.

It's an art to fashion the best parchment
the texture may be too rough or porous,
the colours run and stain into one another
other pages are waxy, impervious
unable to absorb or contain the inks
but the best can hold the precise design.
My skin is fine vellum, I've received your imprint
the sacred indent and the one error, sign
that God alone is the artist without flaw;
love carries cost, the mundane holds awe.

Each knot, each pattern has particular meaning
cross-carpet, curlicue, key and scroll
the four coiled whorl, the weaving plait

the continuous thread that binds the soul
through labyrinth, maze and asymmetry.
The sturdy knots contract or expand
yet hold like a hurdy-gurdy drone;
the spiral winds and unwinds the spirit
from heaven, *the descending gyre*
the three armed treliske is *secret fire.*

Eadfrith penned and illustrated me with extreme skill
Bishop Ethelwald bound me in beech and crimson goatskin
Billfrith the Anchorite adorned me with gold and jewels
Aldred the Glossator translated me into Anglo-Saxon.
My home sacked by Vikings, I wandered seven years
my seven Bearers fled for Ireland, a storm groaned:
three great waves swept the ship, and turned to blood,
I was washed overboard and lost, the voyage abandoned;
but St Cuthbert appeared to Hunred, and told him where
I could be found, at low tide, washed intact to shore.

To The Hermitage
Island of Hvar, Croatia

The bay pulses in concentric rings
the water washes over a fish-eyed jetty;
a blue bowl deep with sky and sun,
sea braces against stone.

Drawn by the dragnet of birdsong
I'm walking to the Hermitage of Hvar
over dry red earth, past bee-thick shrubs,
giant bees, bees inside buttercups.

Flowers grow profuser and richer:
purple petunias nod flimsy heads
yellow prickly gorse, dog roses, fire-stars
mauve menorahs and scarlet pimpernels.

There. On a rock outcrop, alone,
mastering the sea, stands a tiny chapel,
pink plaster and a peeling green door;
a vineyard spreads to the shore's edge.

My heart beats faster, a gladness grows,
in the cool shadow my prayer goes out.
There is the rose of attar, the utter blue
the peace and silence I've been waiting for.

Fish shoals shudder the clear water
I want to bring the world into this blue.

Prisoners of Conscience Windows
Five lancet windows by Gabriel Loire, Salisbury Cathedral.

*Let the lie come into the world, even dominate the world,
But not through me.* (Solzenhitzyn)

Blue

Once
I wept
for myself alone;
now I weep for
others, infinite blues
that intone jagged
litanies; deep blues,
bled from other blues
against Sarum stone.

Black

There
are still
those who
choose Truth
over living the lie;
who measure the stake
and consider the price
not too high; black jet
dense intensity, tightens
inside: *I won't give any
more power to the Lie!*

Red

Ruby
stains the
glass shards;
blood, bitterness;
between barbed wire
soldered, grooved,
leaded, curved;
a chalice catches
the drops of fear;
pigment melts in
the furnace, in this
agony of love, this fire.

Green

Wait
in solitude,
self-questioning
deprived of movement
and light; doubt like
poisoned dart skewers
but the Anchor of hope
tugs on endless night;
in the morning, like birds
upon the sill, soft green
wings of prayers alight.

Gold

The
King
is stretched
out to die;
God's Gold
showers his head;
glory irradiates darkness;
translucent light pierces
the martyrs' graves;
resurrection ascends,
a white spiral.

World's End

There are maps of that old country
creased and stained, prized by a few
there are tokens, markings, clues
however, the dimension is other
the manner of entrance is secret
but not lost, hidden nor unknowable.

Even though imagination was paling
the hope of that country persevered
for those who lived underground
there were inklings, reverberations
travellers came with stirring tales:
were they heralds, sirens or fools?

As though from a long way away
as in a dream, as one blind
in the whiteness of snow
I came slowly, believing, unbelieving
I was drawn as though by the summoning
of great bronze bells beneath the sea...

All of a sudden it was there – the door
that opens onto the edge of the world
I went through that opening of brightness
as though through a gap in the clouds

And it was all so easy
to be on the other side
it was not possible that there could be
any other place to be.

From outside,
all strains towards that dim doorway
all is staked on that one way out;
once there
you can no longer see how you entered

*and it is hard to imagine why
you were not always there nor
how you should ever return whence you came.*

So it was I came into a land of fullness
where laughter is spreading in endless rings
where the Beloved is and the heart's desire
and none of anything else matters at all;
for each one is finding his own story
each becoming what he was meant to be.

There strength seized hold of me
and the skill of sweetness
my wounds became my healing
I came to inhabit my own space
the distances of understanding grew as
the land pushed out its boundaries in me.

I knew I could stay there for ever
that there was much more, so much!
But soon my body was falling back
unable to hold the vision for long;
the grassy land faded away to earth
and the doorway disappeared to human eye.

Yet the taste of that country remained
and I knew I could always return
as effortlessly as the child
closing its eyes into sleep
and as hard as the breaking of dawn
to those who live in night.

Pine Stretching Cloud Sea
Huangshan, Yellow Mountains, China

We two, together almost thirty years,
pass without pause over the *Bridge of Padlocks*.

Here at *Beginning-to-Believe Peak*,
what's left is the fragrance of wet ferns.

The stealth of mist reveals, conceals,
tranquillity begins to spread like wild magnolia.

Below us, trees with bouquets of golden thread plum,
japonica and jade-white quatrefoil dogwood.

Yesterday we walked eight kilometers
today, walking backwards downhill, brings less pain.

The *Umbrella Pine* stretches out its arms of welcome
its handlebar branch bristles green and auburn whiskers.

When the mist parts, there are pinnacles never seen
each viewing point a precipice edge.

Unknown white flowers cling to the cleft of cliff
the smallest plant is worth protecting.

You share your fears, cares and longing for Home
the mountain watches, a great beating heart.

Here, an etiquette of attention and kindness;
the gracefulness of *Pine Stretching Cloud Sea*. ⁄⁄

The Gale

Astringent wind flays trees, flails branches
rakes reeds, rattles windows, doors, skin
knocks everything out of place and beat.
All latches and catches jostle and jig.
It hushes only to gather up a new roar,
crops are blasted, memories dazed.

The waters have overflowed their banks
pale milky green, the river roils,
rises then splits into ribs, scallops, chevrons;
two bedraggled swans breast the oncoming waves.

The coat of grass smarts, prickles –
nerves in the teeth of the metal trap.
Arteries and veins are engorged,
boulders bruised, earth grazed.

Sleeping sickness swaddles the land
spreads its dragnets, stifles strength
fatigue hits like a hammer, an ache
of sleep that can never be slept out.

Yet pussy willow nods on twig tips
tiny leaves blade from brown trees
brave green buds jut from their sheath
crushed glass blue bones dance.

The pelt of snowdrops gives way to crocuses
daffodils open, close and re-open
guests dressed up in silver and gold
for a long-delayed wedding feast.

Birdsong pierces in sweet loneliness,
rejoicing, poised on the cusp
earth's body pangs, in breech labour
waiting for breakthrough.

Yellow Panic Bird

He doesn't get it that she gets this nervousness;
she can't explain it because she doesn't understand it
and he certainly doesn't feel it,
he doesn't know, he just doesn't know.
He's been away just that bit longer than she can bear,
he greets her briefly, they're not alone
she goes and waits for him in their room –
he doesn't come, he does not come.

Then the yellow Panic Bird comes,
it's absurd, she knows it's absurd,
but still it comes – large, livid and yellow
flaps its wings, caws from a huge beak,
tries to smother, claw open her chest –
her heart is red, raw and trembling
she cries, shakes and wrenches –
it's absurd, she knows it's out of proportion.

She wants him to come and hold her,
to sweep her away; he doesn't come.
He'll come later – he has no idea how she feels
he'll be cross because she's needy and demanding
and she's needy because he is always going away.
There is no end to this cycle.
The love they were in, the vows under God –
have to mean something, don't they?

So she's caught in a vice,
her breath gasps, heart beats wildly
the panic comes and she can't stop it
she's aroused – *Don't torment me!* she pleads
silently – *Stop this, I want this to stop!*
At last he comes to her, alone
honey-voiced, pliant, bearing gifts,
his labour construed as love in action.

They embrace, she is shocked by the feel of him,
so new and unfamiliar, though known.
She's intoxicated by the smell of his skin,
the soft warmth of his mouth.
They embrace and she wonders –
*How can she embrace this man who tears her
apart every time? Again and again.
How is it possible to live this way?*

He leaves. Too soon. Before time.
A twenty-four hour snatched visit. They embrace.
A cry breaks out in her, she can't prevent it.
He gets upset with her,
his guilt makes him unkind.
How can they part like this?
And yet they do. Once again.
Over and over.

From her room she sees him go,
marching out in his red fleece top
with suitcase and briefcase;
he's leaving, he's steeled himself
he's flying to Pristina, to the mountains,
snow and dirt, rubbish on the streets,
to his rented room from where he'll phone her,
sounding misplaced and lonely.

When he's gone she wears his sweatshirt –
blue and grey striped, fine wool,
it smells of spicy aftershave,
holds him still close around her.
The yellow panic bird comes, small and feeble now;
she remembers how he loves her but cannot stay;
he must work, it's just bad fate, that's all.

He found his niche in the war-zones
rebuilding bombed towns, mined villages
always on the move, planning structures,
houses, a Palace of Justice, football stadium,

schools, hospitals, bridges – worthy causes.
Their children stay with her for school and safety.
You love a man like this how do you live with him?
She retrieves him from a land beyond seeing. ⁄⁄

Don't

Don't sit with the door ajar
where a sudden gust might change your temperature

Don't walk in the new-cut grass
and smell its heady scent

Don't feel the sweep of willow across your face
watch bees fly from yellow heart to heart

Don't follow the bird flying to the beyond
or dream with clouds changing shape

Don't sit in the blue wooden summerhouse
where paint and easel lie waiting

Don't waste time, it drains down a hole
there are better things you could be doing

Don't grab the sunlight and walk
along North Beach, the lapping-peace sea

Don't pause at piled up white stones
kids making sandcastles and seaweed faces

Don't sit in the cave of comforting
and cry for things lost and found

Don't welcome the warmth of his face
when he comes late with his hands held up.

The Remedy

If, one day, suddenly, you should know yourself
to be lonely, your heart knotted, alien,
hard-edged, shrunk to a speck;
suspended over something too dark and deep
to contemplate, your body cold,
that you must huddle your arms around.

If you then went to your Dr, he might prescribe this:
that you lie down, next to one you love –
in sleep he would place his arm over your chest
and in your right angle to it, a sensation
of merging into oneness would begin,
not knowing where you begin or end.

Then, you might turn your body to one side
and position your heart next to his
slowly, you'd become aware of your heart beating,
his heart moving beneath yours
and your heart would expand inside its halo;
a glow would spread through your whole being.

After several minutes, hours, days,
your heart would become full enough
to carry this new warmth and wholeness
for a few days and in silence.
Knitted and sewn together
seamless.

And you might place your head in the crook
of his shoulder and nuzzle into place.
You'd remember you were once connected to your mother
in the womb and before that to the universe –
in which you live and move
and to which you will return.

Painting Jordan
A poem written backwards

I

Just beneath the surface
swerving always out of reach
a shoal of silver and blue minnows

Yellow and black striped flounders
rainbow fish, dull orange sponges
black spiked sea urchins on the seabed

Underwater, the *Coral Garden*
is the only place to be
it's hot, unbearably burning, lethal

Pale turquoise, malachite green
lapiz lazuli blue, three distinct bands
the Red Sea: *Aqaba.*

II

Lavender, puce, orange ochre, butterscotch
terracotta, tawny, mushroom
only merge with the colours of sand.

Only the pull and burst of the stars
no demands, only here and now
no time or age, no place, only space.

Small, splayed legs, elegant
seven cream camels amble
a campfire burns frankincense resin.

Sunset, blood red, behind indigo hills
peach sand with pale orange stripes.
Barefoot walking, it's an immersion.

The fields of Mars, dune drifts,
a Bedouin tent at Lawrence Canyon,
desert valley: *Wadi Rum*.

III

Jack Sparrow originals
with goatee, dagger, bandana headscarf
Bedouin men with kohl-lined eyes.

Psychedelic graffiti
horizontal mauve humbug stripes
molten toffee spilling over.

Sudden, the Treasury pillared facade
through water-hollowed twisted stone,
along a shaded canyon gorge.

A crown in a mouth of ivory
an old gold shiny stone
amidst a cobbled pathway.

Burnt sienna, powder blue, ochre
apricot, dove-grey, dusty pink:
Rose City in mysterious ruins: *Petra.*

Tavern of the Troubadours
Sintra, Portugal

Every weekend he hosts this space
Queen bee of the thrumming hive,
keeping live music alive, musicians old and new
stock still, holding high his Spanish guitar
he keeps a very strong beat
the rhythm is the constant undercurrent
his crusty bread voice, sometimes shreds
like waves on the crest, breaking.

The *Fado* singer leans in to the hub
tilts her face in to the mic
her voice, clear as a bell
trembles to the song's meaning;
the pianist picks it up, carries
her lilt on mellow velvet keys.

The accordionist sways, a man in love
his music box, a jewelled breastplate;
just before the end, the trumpeter wakes,
croons a muffled tapered sweetness.

It's way too late, but we've forgotten time
along with Merlot, Gaelic coffee and candleflame,
music is a meal made with skill and care
we are also leaning, buzzing, crying from the belly
we love and weep with the troubadours
who are still keeping the heartbeat alive.

Blue Saxophone

Reborn
as the life that emerges
from the chrysalis

its skin still soft and drowsy
the huddled, humming notes

slowly come into consciousness
to form their own shape, the sound

that springs from the belly of an azure saxophone
out through the bell of its throat

golden acorns cluster in the base,
jostle up the U and flick beads and husks

then stream together into a melody
that chatters, skitters, lollops, sprints,

brims over like children let out of school.
A sweetwater spring that bubbles and blips

up, out and away
into vertical waves of liquid blue.

Acknowledgements

'Sarajevo' first appeared in *Dreamcatcher*, Balkan Edition

'Alfred Jewel' and 'Woman' appeared in *In the Gold of Flesh*, The Women's Press.

'World's End' appeared in *Into the Farther Reaches*, Avalon.

'Blue Saxophone' appeared in *The People's Psalms*, Arrowriver.

'Blue Turtle' and 'The Dissident' appeared in *Flame Songs*, Subtle Flame.

'Lamentation' was translated into Macedonian by Irena Andreevski and appeared in *The Door*, Skopje.

'The House', 'Day of Wind' and 'Gale' appeared in Linley Hill Poems.

'Rothko Room' and 'Spring' appeared in *Beneath the Surface*, Subtle Flame.

'The Dissident' appeared in *Causeway*, Arrowriver.

'Prisoners of Conscience Windows' and 'Walking to the House of Song' appeared in *Small Candles*, Amnesty International.

'Carefully Fall to the River' appeared in *Healing Nature*, Full Circle Collective.

'Sarajevo', 'WW1 Memoir' and 'The Dissident' are to appear in *Olive Branch, Poems for Peace*, Ground.

Other anthologies and collections available from Stairwell Books

Exiles	Ilmar Lehtpere
Village Fox	Richard Cave
An Anxiety of Poets in their Natural Habitat	Amina Alyal
First of All I Wrote Your Name	Winston Plowes
Sleeve Heart	Eleanor May Blackburn
Goldfish	Jonathan Aylett
Strike	Sarah Wimbush
Marginalia	Doreen Hinchliffe
The Estuary and the Sea	Jennifer Keevill
In | Between	Angela Arnold
Quiet Flows the Hull	Clint Wastling
Lunch on a Green Ledge	Stella Davis
there is an england	Harry Gallagher
Iconic Tattoo	Richard Harries
Herdsmenization	Ngozi Olivia Osuoha
On the Other Side of the Beach, Light	Daniel Skyle
Words from a Distance	Ed. Amina Alyal, Judi Sissons
Fractured	Shannon O'Neill
Unknown	Anna Rose James, Elizabeth Chadwick Pywell
When We Wake We Think We're Whalers from Eden	Bob Beagrie
Awakening	Richard Harries
Starspin	Graehame Barrasford Young
A Stray Dog, Following	Greg Quiery
Steel Tipped Snowflakes 1	Izzy Rhiannon Jones, Becca Miles, Laura Voivodeship
Where the Hares Are	John Gilham
The Glass King	Gary Allen
Gooseberries	Val Horner
Poetry for the Newly Single 40 Something	Maria Stephenson
Northern Lights	Harry Gallagher
More Exhibitionism	Ed. Glen Taylor
The Beggars of York	Don Walls
Lodestone	Hannah Stone
Learning to Breathe	John Gilham
Throwing Mother in the Skip	William Thirsk-Gaskill
New Crops from Old Fields	Ed. Oz Hardwick
The Ordinariness of Parrots	Amina Alyal
Homeless	Ed. Ross Raisin
Somewhere Else	Don Walls
York in Poetry Artwork and Photographs	Ed. John Coopey, Sally Guthrie

For further information please contact rose@stairwellbooks.com

www.stairwellbooks.co.uk

www.ingramcontent.com/pod-product-compliance
Lightning Source LLC
Chambersburg PA
CBHW051716040426
42446CB00008B/908